BLESS
AND BE
BLESSED

BLESS AND BE BLESSED

How Your Words Can Make a Difference

PETER M. LORD

FOREWORD BY ADRIAN ROGERS

Revell
Grand Rapids, Michigan

© 2004 by Peter M. Lord

Published by Fleming H. Revell
a division of Baker Book House Company
P.O. Box 6287, Grand Rapids, MI 49516-6287
www.bakerbooks.com

Printed in the United States of America

Library of Congress Cataloging-in-Publication Data
Lord, Peter, 1929-
    Bless and be blessed : how your words can make a difference / Peter M. Lord ;
  foreword by Adrian Rogers.
        p.   cm.
    Includes bibliographical references.
    ISBN 0-8007-5937-0 (pbk.)
    1. Praise—Religious aspects—Christianity. 2. Blessing and cursing. I. Title.
BV4597.53.P73L67 2004
241'.672—dc22   2003027010

To my friends who always saw more in me than I did in myself, and who regularly let me know it: Joe Boatwright, Gary Kirksey, and Mickey Evans. Their encouragement has meant far more to me than they will know this side of eternity. Thanks, men.

A special thank you
To Van Savell, whose editorial skills and good suggestions made this book possible, and

To all the good people at Baker Book House, with whom it's been so easy and pleasurable to work.

CONTENTS

Foreword by Adrian Rogers   9
Introduction Miraculous Life Changes   11

Part 1   Can I Really Bless Others?

1. The Discovery of This Truth   19
2. Why Blessings Are So Powerful   25
3. A Very Negative World   33
4. An Important Fact to Remember   39
5. The Time for Blessing Is Now   47
6. Is This Really Biblical?   53
7. What You Should Know about Blessings   63
8. Two Levels of Power in Blessings   71

Part 2   How Can I Bless Others?

9. Developing the Ability to Bless   79
10. Accepting Our Blessings from God   91
11. Enjoying Our Relationship with God   95
12. Receiving Our Inheritance from God   103
13. Living in God's Provision   109

Part 3 Where Do I Start?

14. Simple Ways to Give Blessings   121
15. How to Begin and What to Say   133

Conclusion Simple yet Powerful Words   139
Notes   141

FOREWORD

Some books are mere books, and others are transformational books. Believe me when I tell you that this volume by Peter Lord is transformational.

When I first received the manuscript, I could not put it down until I had gone through to the last page. When I finished reading, thoughts began to fire off in my mind and heart. I said to myself, *Adrian, you need to put this into practice in a greater way in your life.* Then I thought of my children and said to myself, *I want my children to read this book.* I told Joyce, my wife, "You will love Peter's new book."

Peter Lord has a mind that is incisive and a great heart that cares for people. These gifts enable him to speak with a freshness and penetrating insight that make his teaching relevant, practical, and biblical. This volume speaks of a quality that we all need—encouragement. If we say we do not need encouragement or do not want it, we are probably not telling the truth. Yet we have all found that it seems easier to criticize than to speak well of others. It does not take much to criticize.

May this book cause all of us to obey the Scriptures and speak well of one another.

Most likely you will not pass this book on. Why? You will want to keep it for yourself, but doubtless you will want to purchase others to give to friends.

Read it and be blessed and also be a blessing.

Adrian Rogers
Senior Pastor
Bellevue Baptist Church
Memphis, Tennessee

MIRACULOUS LIFE CHANGES

Gary was such a hell raiser in the seventh and eighth grades his principal hoped he wouldn't return to school for ninth grade, but he did.

On the first day of that school year, he was ordered to a counselor's office. There the counselor talked with Gary. As a result, Gary excelled that year, receiving honors for his work and behavior. He is now a pastor of a church in Lubbock, Texas. Gary credits what was said to him as the beginning of his changed life and behavior.

What did the counselor say to him? The same basic things that were said to a matriarch in a church:

Pastor Joe had incurred the wrath of a woman in his church, who over the years had obtained much power. She would not speak to his wife and seldom spoke to him. One day Pastor Joe sat down and wrote her a note. (By his own admission his pride prevented him from mailing it for a few weeks.) After receiving the note, the matriarch became a different person. Her attitude toward the pastor and his family completely changed.

What did he say in this note? The same basic things said to another troubled student:

Bill was in the seventh grade in a private school. His behavior was such that the principal was constantly on the phone with his parents. One day a school employee called Bill's father and talked with him about his son. The father told his son why the school had called. Later the school principal said that from that day forward the boy's behavior changed dramatically.

What did that school employee say? The same things said to an American Airlines employee:

An official at a Texas airport was having difficulty with the work ethic of an employee. No matter what the official said or threatened, the work habits of the employee didn't seem to change. But one day the official spoke certain words to the worker, and in three days the man became a model employee. He even began coming to his supervisor and asking for more work.

What did the supervisor say that made such a difference? The same things that were said to an unhappy worker:

As a Christmas gift Debbie wrote a note to all her team members. After the holidays one member of her team told her he had been planning to quit at the beginning of the new year, but her letter had changed his mind. He now planned to continue working.

What did she write? The same basic things that were said to a discouraged university student:

As a professor sat in his car on campus, he noticed a student with a discouraged look. Dr. Tommy called the student over and spoke to him. Three days later the student showed up in the professor's office and explained that he had been on his way home to pack up and quit school when the professor had spoken to him. Now he was staying in school and planning for the future.

What was said that made such a difference? The same basic things that Jewish children hear:

As a matter of tradition, Jewish parents spur their children on to great success. What they say has such an effect on them that in the United States there are fewer Jews in jail and more successful Jews in high places than members of any other ethnic group. Percentage-wise Jews are awarded more Nobel and Pulitzer prizes than any other group of people.

What do their parents do or say that makes such a difference?

Many more stories could be told of the transformations that have come to people through words spoken to them. What words? What do all these stories have in common? What magic words are used to bring about such transformations? Some of the actual things said will be mentioned later on, but for now we will consider what the messages all had in common.

The words that were said were positive, encouraging words. Our English Bible translations call them "blessings." At funerals they are called "eulogies." Yes, eulogies—the nice stuff they say about folks at funerals with, of course, one major difference. In the stories above, the recipients of the eulogies were still alive. Some of them were barely teenagers; some, like the church matriarch, were older. All of them heard or read good, kind, encouraging words that focused on their positive characteris-

13

tics. And the best part is these people could hear their eulogies because they were still alive.

The intent of this book is to call us back to the biblical concept of blessing people, speaking well of them. Among the many things God is, he is a blesser. Satan, on the other hand, is known as the "accuser of the brethren."

We are called to live in harmonious relationships, to bless rather than insult. Peter said we were called for this very purpose (see 1 Peter 3:9).

Is it your desire to be a blessing to those around you? This book will help you do just that. Each of the following chapters ends with a suggested "blessing exercise." If you do these exercises and carry out the other suggestions in this book, you will be well on your way to becoming a blessing to everyone around you.

PART ONE

CAN I REALLY BLESS OTHERS?

Papa, I don't have money to buy presents this year, so I am going to write a note to everyone.

Thank you for showing me all the things about life that you do; thank you for the way you disciple me. You have really shown me what it is to live your life for Jesus, and how to bite the bullet even when it seems very hard.

Thank you for letting me live in your house. You have really showed me how to live life the right way, and I do not know if I can ever repay you for what you have done for me.

I love you very much and will do anything I can around the house to help out.

Merry Christmas.

Love,
Richie

On Christmas Day 2002 I received this note from my grandson, a college student who lives with us. It is more valuable to me than any material present I could have received.

ONE

THE DISCOVERY
OF THIS TRUTH

As a pastor for fifty years, I heard many eulogies, but they were always associated with funerals, when a friend or loved one was complimented posthumously. I can never remember a bad word said about any person at a funeral. At times it seemed as if the deceased had become a supersaint between the day of his or her death and the memorial service.

Just because it's traditional to give eulogies after a person has died doesn't mean it's the right time, and it doesn't mean we can't change a long engrained habit. If we are willing to learn a new way of doing things, we are never too old to do so. At least, that's the way it has worked for me.

Bill Ligon, a pastor in Brunswick, Georgia, discovered the secret of blessings. Through their use, he saw many lives changed. As he taught others about blessings, they reported back to him life-changing testimonials. Eventually he wrote the book *Imparting the Blessing to Your Children: What the Jewish Patriarchs Knew*.

Here's a little of what he wrote:

> God planned for life to be imparted through the spoken blessing. The Old Testament fathers expected the blessing to release God's favor into their lives and the lives of their children. That same expectation can rest in the hearts of all who accept the challenge to learn the biblical way to bless.[1]

To supplement his book, Ligon has produced a series of taped messages detailing the blessing concept. It includes how to have a blessing service in church for adults or children.

Bill Glass, a former professional football player, directs one of the largest prison ministries in the country. A statement in one of his audiotapes really grabbed my attention. He said, "One year there were sixty thousand inmates in Florida prisons and only thirteen Jews."[2]

As a resident of Florida, I know we have a large Jewish population. This unusually small percentage of prisoners really impressed me. Glass attributes this astoundingly low number to the way Jewish parents take the time to verbally bless their children on a regular basis.

Some time ago two audiotapes and a very small book were sent to me, all three arriving within days of each other. To this day I am not sure how I got them. I listened to the tapes and soon after read the book. They were all on the subject of the power of blessings.

The book, by Dr. Mary Ruth Swope, a Texas nutritionist, was *Bless Your Children Every Day*. In the introduction Dr. Swope explained how she discovered the power of blessing through the testimony of a Baptist pastor who had been fired. Here is the testimony:

> Shocked over the dismissal and brokenhearted by the aftermath of events, the pastor was depressed and lonely. To make matters worse, many of the other clergymen in his area shunned him, leaving him feeling devastated.
>
> A few days later, however, one of his good friends—the local Jewish rabbi—came to express his sadness over the unfortunate affair. "I want to do more than extend my condolences," the rabbi said. "I've come to bless you."
>
> Those words took on deep spiritual meaning as the rabbi shared with the pastor the traditions of the Jewish faith regarding blessings. "I believe God's blessings on Jewish people is a direct result of Jewish parents regularly blessing their children," the rabbi said, noting that a majority of all Nobel and Pulitzer Prizes have been awarded to Jewish men and women. And also a large percentage of America's millionaires are Jewish people, and yet they comprise only 2.7 percent of the population.
>
> As a result of the rabbi's visit, the pastor began to study this phenomenon of blessing in the Scriptures. Before long, he started teaching other fathers to daily bless their spouses and children, opening many new doors of ministry for him throughout the country.[3]

I have learned that most truth comes in seed form, and, if the seed is received and cultivated, it brings forth a great harvest. So, on receiving this seed of truth, I immediately began to put it into practice, for I also had discovered that if neglected, the truth is very soon forgotten.

Our English word *eulogy* comes directly from the Greek language and is made up of two words, *eu* meaning well, and *logos* meaning word. Together, they convey the idea of a good word. It is interesting to note also that the Latin word for bless is *benedicere*, which also means to say good things. So there is a close connection in meaning between *blessing* and *eulogy*.

Unfortunately, in our language and culture, the eulogy is associated only with funerals. The idea of eulogy, saying good things, is completely consistent with the meaning of the word, but it seems unfortunate that those good words are said about a person primarily after he or she dies.

In John 12 we find the story of Mary of Bethany anointing Jesus with expensive perfume: "Then Mary took about a pint of pure nard, an expensive perfume; she poured it on Jesus' feet and wiped his feet with her hair" (v. 3). Some of the people who were present criticized Mary for the waste of the perfume. Ronald Rolheiser comments:

> There is great irony here. If a woman had gone to Jesus' tomb with this outpouring of affection and perfume, it would have been accepted, even admired. You were allowed to anoint a dead body, but it was not acceptable to express similar love and affection to a live one. Nothing has changed in two thousand years. We still save our best compliments and flowers for the funeral. Jesus' challenge here is for us to anoint each other while we are still alive. Shower those you love with affection and flowers while they are alive, not at their funerals.[4]

Remember, no matter what you say or think about a person, if the only time it is said is at his or her funeral, the person never hears a word of it.

A BLESSING EXERCISE

Speak a "good word" to someone today.

ALL The Time

December 25, 2002

Dear Dad:

I wanted you to know the following things.

1. You have made the most positive changes in yourself in the last ten years. You have broken down many barriers, with improved communication, listening, and positive praise.

2. You have been an inspiration to me as I have tried to follow your wise counsel and advice. The more I have listened to you and applied it, the more successful I have become.

3. You have been so generous to Ruth Ann and me in so many areas. You and Mother have blessed us so much with your calls, visits, and gifts. Your eulogies to me have greatly affected me.

A eulogy from a son-in-law

TWO

WHY BLESSINGS ARE
SO POWERFUL

The power of blessing is evident through what blessings accomplish. When good words are spoken to us, they meet some of our most basic needs, needs that every person has, put there by our Creator.

The Christian life is basically walked out on the two legs of our God-image and self-image. Our God-image is what we think of God—what we think he is like and what he approves and disapproves. Our self-image or identity is what we believe God and others think of us. If either one of these is seriously damaged, or if either one is false, our spirit is affected, and we limp through life.

This damage may result from things that happen in childhood or youth. Many people have their self-image skewed because of what significant people said to them in the past. Often parents can cause the damage in early life; spouses may be responsible later.

The distorted God-image—our idea of what God is really like—may be caused by what others have communicated to us about God. Gradually our God-image may become only a caricature of the true God. Then it's difficult to think of God as a loving heavenly Father and to establish a personal relationship with him.

The Scriptures warn us not to think too highly of ourselves but to think soberly and rightly (see Rom. 12:3). But for every person who thinks too highly of himself or herself, there are a hundred who think too little of themselves. Most people believe that God thinks significantly less of them than what God actually thinks. To think too little of oneself is not humility but a form of inverted pride, because it is not thinking "soberly and rightly" but negatively and it is prideful because it is self-centered.

How God Made Us

God created us with needs. God could have made us without needs, but he didn't. Not only did God create us with needs, he provided the means by which all these needs can legitimately be met. Temptation is nothing more than the enticement to meet a legitimate need in an illegitimate way or a God-given need in a God-forbidden way. God has forbidden us to meet given needs in certain ways because he knows in the long run those choices will hurt us.

It should not be surprising that God wants to meet many of our God-created needs. He designed many others, however, to be met through our interaction with other people, especially by the significant people in our lives—those who are close to us, such as family, friends, coworkers, and those we admire and respect for one reason or another. When people are important to us, we value what they say and their words can greatly affect us.

Good words from the significant people in our lives are very important to each of us. Good words can come from many sources, however. And, regardless of who speaks them to us, they can be a blessing.

We can understand the power of eulogies when we understand how God made us and some of the natural soul needs he created within us. Just as we need physical food for physical growth and sustenance, we also need soul food—special attention from God and others.

We were made in the image and likeness of God, who desires and wants our praise. So it is natural for us to need and want praise too. The psalmist said we are to enter God's gates with thanksgiving and his courts with praise (Ps. 100:4). Similarly, when we interact with people and when we enter the "gates" of others, it is good to come with praise or eulogies.

It will shock many people to hear or see these words: God is not enough. But it was God who said it first. Before sin entered into the world, God the Creator said to Adam, "It is not good for the man to be alone" (Gen. 2:18). So God created a companion and helper, Eve.

We have needs that can be met only by proper interaction with others. The need for a supportive family is basic, but help can also come from people outside our family. In a world with so many dysfunctional families, where the needs of many are not being met, it is incumbent on the family of God to function properly, satisfying people's needs for healthy and satisfying relationships.

Real Soul Food

One of the ways to feed our souls is with words. Words, just like regular food, can be good or bad. If good, they build us up; if bad, they can devastate us.

Jesus said, "Man does not live on bread alone, but on every word that comes from the mouth of God" (Matt. 4:4). God's words come to his people directly through the Bible or indirectly through men and women like you and me. God has asked us to speak on his behalf; we are challenged to minister to others by speaking good words. When our world is filled with negative and destructive words, it can be our happy privilege to counter the negative with positive, edifying words.

Remember: Good soul food is good words, and bad soul food is bad words.

To live a full and meaningful life
every person needs to receive
good words
from other people.

When we receive on a regular basis certain kinds of feedback from others, we can be whole people. Our spirit needs to sense certain positive things as much as our body needs to digest food, and most often we will receive these sentiments through words of:

Appreciation
Acceptance
Approval
Affection
Attention
Affirmation
Admiration

Think of how you feel when you receive words that meet these needs. We can think of them as seven facets of love, ways we can encourage one another and sure ways to develop good relationships.

In the Scriptures there are reciprocal commands that each of us is to obey. When there is reciprocity, each person will give and receive what each craves. One such command is found in Hebrews 3:13: "Encourage one another daily, as long as it is called Today, so that none of you may be hardened by sin's deceitfulness."

Our example in this life, Jesus, received blessings from the Father, who proclaimed, "This is My beloved Son, in whom I am well-pleased" (Matt. 3:17). His Father was the truly significant person in his life. Think of the admiration, affirmation, affection, and approval Jesus received from the One whose opinion was vitally important to him.

When was the last time you deliberately praised or blessed another person? Those who need praise or blessing the most are often the people to whom it is most difficult to give it. Even though the faults of such people may be very prominent, still we must seek to bless them.

A BLESSING EXERCISE

Which of the seven kinds of feedback would you like someone to give you today? Ask God to allow that to happen, for he is eager to meet all our needs in one way or another. Then look for a way to meet the need for that same feedback in someone else.

The tongue has the power of life and death.

Proverbs 18:21

Gentle words bring life and health.

Proverbs 15:4 NLT

Your own soul is nourished when you are kind, but you destroy yourself when you are cruel.

Proverbs 11:17 NLT

THREE

A VERY NEGATIVE WORLD

Think with me about the impact of our society.

- What do teachers mark on kids' papers at school?— the wrong answers.
- Has a policeman ever stopped you and thanked you for driving courteously, for staying in the proper lane, and for stopping at the last ten thousand stop signs?
- Has the government ever written you and thanked you for paying taxes?
- When an authority figure calls you in, do you expect rebuke or commendation?

- Have you noticed that if you do a hundred good things and one bad thing, it is usually only the bad thing that is remembered and mentioned?
- How often do your children thank you for all you've done and are doing for them? Even when they are grown up, don't they usually recall the occasional mistakes you made in parenting rather than the good things you did on a regular basis?

We live in a very negative world, where negative things have power and prominence. Read the newspaper or watch the evening news on TV. The negative gets top billing, makes the headlines. In our personal lives this is also true. It is easier for us to see the negative than the positive. We have a strong tendency to judge others, and sometimes we not only judge them, we also pass some kind of sentence on them.

When you think about what a negative world we live in, your mind soon goes to political campaigning, in which, rather than presenting one's own platform, the basic tactic is to call attention to flaws in the opposition's character and actions. The candidate may have promised not to run a negative campaign—even though the opponent may stoop to mudslinging, he or she will never do such a thing but will run a positive campaign. That usually lasts for about two weeks. Soon the ads on TV and in the newspapers are disgustingly negative. Both candidates are slinging mud, and the voters wish they didn't have to vote for either one.

In our law courts, the usual tactic is to question a person's character, pointing out his or her inabilities, failures, and mistakes. The idea is to do all you can to discredit your opponent in every way possible. The divorce courts of the nation are notorious for this. Once a couple was in love and saw and said nothing but good about each other, but when they get to divorce court, they expose every negative thing imaginable.

■ The Effect of Negative Words

Counselors see the effects of negative words in one client after another. They see firsthand the damage a few negative words can do. Even when the negative words were spoken many years earlier, they cannot be erased, especially when a very significant person in the person's life, like a mother or father, uttered them.

My wife counseled an older person, a woman who had recently retired. Her job was significant and she had excelled in her field. Yet she was still held in bondage by something negative her father had said fifty years earlier. In the heart of an impressionable child a few discouraging words have great and lasting power.

Though we live in a very negative world, negativity doesn't apply at funerals. Funerals are the exception. In fact a funeral is about the only place where nothing negative is ever said.

After a notoriously wicked man in Texas died, his brother tried to find a minister who would conduct the funeral and say somewhere in the message, "This man was a saint." However, the man's reputation was so bad no pastor wanted to conduct the service. Finally, when the brother offered one thousand dollars to the minister who would do it, one pastor jumped at the opportunity.

The church was crowded. Many were wondering how the pastor would handle the brother's request. At one point in the service, the minister paused, looked down at the casket and then out at the congregation. With a somber face, he commented, "Compared with his brother, this man was a saint."

■ Offsetting the Negative

How much positive does it take to offset one negative? I personally can't say, but most counselors know from experience that it takes a great deal. One has said that it takes thirty-seven positives to offset one negative in the heart of a child.

I remember an old song from the 1940s. It went like this: "You've got to accentuate the positive, eliminate the negative" and "don't mess with Mister In-Between." Well, we as a society haven't followed that advice. But we can do something about it in our own little world. We need to remember that the darker the night the brighter the light—our positive words and attitudes will stand out in a world of negativism.

In life today a few people get more than they need, but most of us do not get enough and many get nothing. The people at the top, a Michael Jordan, a Tiger Woods, a Bill Gates, are multi-millionaires, not just in money but in the ability that enables them to make the money. As a result, their peers, the fans, and the media heap praise on them.

But most of us are ordinary people, like the single mother who is a waitress at a restaurant, or a clerk in a convenience store, or a sanitation worker. The grounds keeper of the championship course needs praise as much as Tiger Woods does. Probably few golfers give him or her a thought, much less a thanks for the condition of the course. And who remembers to thank the janitor at the school for his or her hard work? The behind-the-scenes worker needs praise as much as the school principal does. We ordinary people need praise, but we seldom get it.

A BLESSING EXERCISE

Speak a word of encouragement to a salesperson today.

There are men who make every man feel small, but the really great man is the man who makes every man feel great.

G. K. Chesterton

The measure of a truly great man is the courtesy with which he treats lesser men.

Anonymous

There is a saying:

If you roll out the red carpet for a billionaire, he will not
    notice it;
for a millionaire, he expects it;
for a thousandaire, he will thank you for it;
but if you do this for a hundredaire (which most of us are),
he will tell everybody about it.

FOUR

AN IMPORTANT FACT
TO REMEMBER

Remember this: If positive feedback is not given, the negative will automatically be assumed. That's the kind of world we live in. Here's an example. If you tell your wife that you love her or how great she is, and she doesn't respond, you automatically assume that something is wrong. You wonder if you offended her when you meant your words to be a compliment. You wonder if she thinks you have a hidden agenda and that you really didn't mean those words at all. This is part of the power of a negative world. We assume the worst not the best.

How to Accentuate the Positive

Let's see how our seven kinds of positive feedback can accentuate what is good in a negative world.

Appreciation

Appreciation is the simple act of recognizing the good in others and acknowledging it. A simple thank-you can work wonders. According to surveys, the most common complaint of workers in America is not about pay but about the lack of appreciation from their employers. If no appreciation is given, employees question their worth and wonder if their work is really valued. Whether it is in the office, the home, or the church, saying a sincere thank-you is always in good taste.

I read a story of a woman who said her home was changed when her husband began to say thank you for the little things he had always taken for granted. Previously, he had often complained about things not being done around the house. When he began to express appreciation for the things that were done, it made all the difference to his wife, and she began to enjoy doing more, just to please her husband.

Acceptance

Let others know that you accept and admire them. If you don't, they will automatically assume your rejection, whether or not you verbalize it. When people feel they are not wanted and accepted, it is traumatic and soul shattering. Much of our life activity is geared to seeking acceptance. We dress and talk in certain ways and go to certain places and events to be accepted. Often the things we purchase—from cars and homes to foods and hardware—we purchase in an effort to be accepted. We even express certain religious beliefs just to feel accepted.

Approval

Give others your stamp of approval. One of the strongest needs in humans is the need for approval. To accept someone is one thing; to approve of him or her goes a step beyond. We all need to know that we are valued by others. If approval is not expressed, we assume the worst—someone does not approve of us. Small children constantly cry out for the approval of their parents, and, as we grow older, this need for approval does not diminish. If we don't receive it from family, friends, and coworkers, we struggle with our self-image. The approval of others is such a strong force that teenagers who receive approval from the wrong crowd soon become followers of that crowd.

Affection

How do you show affection? Caring, friendliness, and words of love are sure ways to express affection. Without affection in regular doses, people feel unloved. The bumper sticker "Have you hugged your kids today?" is a reminder that the lack of parental affection will negatively affect our children throughout their lives. When parents are affectionate, however, this shapes their children in positive ways. Author and lecturer John Trent has said, "If I had a dollar for every man who told me, 'I guess my parents loved me but I never heard them say so,' I could retire as one of the richest men in America." I don't think there are any scientific studies to prove it, but I have heard it said—and I believe it—we need at least five hugs a day to just stay normal.

41

Attention

Give the gift of attention. A friend told me of a two-year-old who looked forward to the day when the cleaning ladies came each week. He would perform for them, crying out, "At me, yadies, at me!" And they would laugh at him and applaud.

Adults crave attention just as much as children. There is a real ADD—attention deficit disorder—in human relationships. Throughout our lives we spend a great deal of time seeking the attention of others, and more and more it seems that we are incapable of giving our undivided attention to someone else. This is probably because we are so taken up with ourselves. Because we want the spotlight on us and our needs, we don't attend to the needs of others, especially if those needs lie just below the surface. Author Jim Rohn says, "One of the greatest gifts you can give to anyone is the gift of attention."

Affirmation

Learn to affirm. It doesn't take a lot of effort, but the rewards of affirming others are great. People are seeking your affirmation; without it, their souls are withering. You speak words of affirmation when you say things like: "I have noticed what a kind person you are." "You have a wonderful smile." "You responded so well to that irritable customer."

Think of how you feel when you don't receive affirmation for your efforts. You begin to assume that what you do is inferior and that you are not worth much. Many people, maybe even a majority of people, suffer from a poor self-image. If they received very little affirmation in childhood, they probably still suffer from that neglect as adults.

Admiration

Start an admiration society. Our self-esteem soars when we are told we are special, and it sinks when a negative thing is said. I am sure that you can remember days when you felt depressed and other days when you felt exhilarated because of what someone said to you. In my own experience a simple compliment about a tie I was wearing encouraged me to wear it often. If two or three people said they liked a tie I wore to the office, I would want to wear it every day for a month!

Admiration is the expression of sincere esteem, whereas flattery is false and insincere praise offered with an ulterior motive. I am not advocating that you practice flattery. Often people will accept deceitful flattery, like rotten food, if there is nothing else available. Though the soul craves good words, it will probably accept false ones, if the good and true ones are not given.

Developing Quality People

In this world quality is very important. That is why the Japanese beat us in the car-selling race. Today American consumers send billions of dollars overseas because we want quality automobiles. In most companies, if you are in charge of quality control, you hold a very important position.

Identifying the inferior and replacing it with the superior is the way to produce quality products. This can be an ongoing process. Products are recalled, and defective or inferior parts are replaced with better parts. When the space shuttle was built, we saw this process in action. The first shuttle was completed at Kennedy Space Center in Florida as a research and development project. Often technicians went home on weekends only to return the next Monday to a whole new concept for bonding the heat shield tiles on the aircraft. When one way of bonding tiles proved unacceptable, they had to develop a whole new process.

Developing quality people is not as easy as developing a quality product, but it is even more important. How is it done? First, we must look for the superior characteristics or actions of people and then commend them for them. Everyone enjoys appreciation, acceptance, approval, affection, attention, affirmation, and admiration, and when we give these responses to people, we help them develop in good ways.

Those of us who are older parents can look back on how we raised our children and we regret that, while we often called attention to our children's weaknesses and faults, we did not praise our children enough for all their good points. Praise is important in the development of a quality person.

A Blessing Exercise

For each form of positive feedback, identify one person who needs to receive it. Attempt to meet this need in each of the seven people this week.

44

One day, when I was in high school, the dean, Carl Price, called me into his office. Frankly I wondered why. Had I done something wrong?

Carl was a large man with a firm but kind expression. He asked, "Adrian, what do you intend to do with your life?"

I said, "Mr. Price, God has called me to be a pastor."

Carl leaned over his desk and said to me, "Adrian, I have been looking at your grades, and they are very average. I have received a record of your IQ score, and it is much higher than average. You are capable of doing much better work than you are doing."

I was a little embarrassed, a little ashamed, but also greatly encouraged. I was encouraged that a man saw potential in me and cared enough about me to confront me. He told me in a loving but forthright way that I could do better.

As a result, my grades began to improve in high school. When I went away to college, my grades were even better. And, when I went to seminary, my grades were still better. As the work got more difficult, my grades improved. I have asked myself why this was the case. I believe sincerely that one of the major reasons was that man cared enough to confront, challenge, and encourage me. I will ever be grateful to Carl Price.

Adrian Rogers

If I treat a person as though he were what he could become, that is what he will become.

FIVE

THE TIME FOR BLESSING IS NOW

The Bible speaks of two people who anointed Jesus. One anointed him with one pound of ointment and the other with seventy-five pounds of ointment. One was Mary; the other was Nicodemus (see Matt. 26:6–13; John 19:38–40). Most people remember the incident of the anointing with the one pound, but hardly any remember the story of Jesus being anointed with a hundred pounds of ointment. Do you know why?

Mary, a former prostitute, had a bottle of perfume that weighed one pound. It was costly perfume, so costly it would have taken a year for a common laborer to earn enough to buy it.

Nicodemus, on the other hand, was a key figure in the city and a member of the Sanhedrin, the group who ruled Israel. A seeker of truth, he was a secret follower of Jesus, and after the crucifixion, he gave seventy-five pounds of ointment to anoint the body of Jesus.

Why is one remembered more than the other? Jesus predicted that what Mary had done would be remembered and told through all the years to come. What was the major difference? It is simply this: One did it while Jesus was alive and the other when Jesus was dead. Mary anointed a living Jesus and Nicodemus a dead Jesus.

Dwight L. Moody said:

> There is a lesson here. How very kind and thoughtful we are to a family who has lost some member, and what kind words are said after the person is dead and gone. Would it not be better to say a few of those good things before they go? Wouldn't it be better to give some of your bouquets before a man dies and not go and load down his coffin with them? He cannot enjoy them then.

My Father's Sermon

My father was a farmer and spoke at church only when circumstances made it absolutely necessary. He was not a good speaker and he knew it. No doubt that was why he hated to stand behind a pulpit and preach. But, as a deacon, he was obligated to preach once in a while in the pastor's absence.

I have forgotten some of his sermons, but I remember one in which he said, "It is better to give a rose to someone when they are alive than a whole wreath when they are dead." I don't know how many thousands of sermons I have heard in my lifetime, and, to tell the truth, I have forgotten almost all of them. But I still remember what my father preached that Sunday.

It strikes me that, if I remembered it for sixty years, it must be very, very important. It has taken me a long time to realize how truly important this message is, but now that I do, it is my aim to give out as many roses as I can while people can appreciate them.

The Johnny Lingo Story

The Johnny Lingo story has been made into a short movie, and it has been told and retold in many publications, but it is worth telling again.

Johnny was a great trader and the richest man in all the Caribbean Islands. Besides this, he was good looking and a very eligible bachelor. All the girls wanted to marry him. In fact he could have had anyone he wanted. No one could understand why he chose Lucita.

A person with the gift of mercy would describe Lucita as plain. That would, in fact, be a very generous description. For years her father had verbally abused her. The marks of a bad self-image and low self-esteem were written all over her.

It was customary on Lucita's island for a man to give a dowry for a wife. The dowry was always in cows. An average bride would bring three cows. Very attractive women were worth four to six cows. Lucita's father knew he would be lucky to get two cows for Lucita, especially because he was up against the smartest trader on the island. So he decided he would ask for two cows and settle for one.

The day of the engagement was a very important day on the island. When Johnny came to ask for Lucita's hand in marriage, the whole community gathered at the home of the bride-to-be. After the necessary introductory formalities, Lucita's father asked Johnny what he was offering for his daughter. Without hesitation Johnny offered eight cows.

The crowd was stunned. Lucita's father could not believe his ears. Had Johnny gone crazy or blind? Why did the smart-

49

est trader in all the islands offer eight cows for someone who could have been had for one? Lucita's father quickly accepted Johnny's offer.

Johnny Lingo and Lucita were married, and in a short period of time, Lucita developed into the most beautiful woman in the islands. The townspeople were amazed at the transformation. So was Lucita's father, who accused Johnny of cheating him. "You should have paid me ten cows," he claimed.

What was Johnny Lingo's secret? What did he know that could transform a person so radically? He had learned that if you treat another person as though she were what she could become, that is what she will become. Johnny wanted an eight-cow wife, so he treated Lucita like one from the beginning.

Isn't this the way God has treated us? Despite our ugliness—our sin—he traded very highly for us. He gave his only Son for us. And now he treats us as his children. This is very hard for us to grasp and accept because of the negative world in which we live, but it illustrates the power of eulogy no matter how it is given.

A BLESSING EXERCISE

Can you recall a time when someone spoke a good word to you that strongly impacted your life? Can you remember doing that for someone else?

God obviously had something in mind for his people when he commanded Moses and Aaron to bless the children of Israel. There is no wasted motion in the activities of God. He does not institute rites as a matter of form. There is purpose behind every movement and activity of God. Every activity he institutes provides life at a higher level than when it is observed.

Bill Ligon

SIX

IS THIS REALLY BIBLICAL?

B y now you are probably wondering: Is this really biblical? What does the Bible have to say about this? The Old Testament was originally written in Hebrew, and when it was translated into Greek, the Septuagint, the translators used the Greek word *eulogy* to translate the Hebrew word *bless.*

I was amazed to find how the word is used in the Bible, and I was even more amazed to see how frequently we are commanded to bless or eulogize. In the Old Testament the word for *bless* is *barak* and appears 330 times, and in the New Testament the word *eulogeo* in its many forms appears 44 times. Jesus used the word quite often. He both practiced giving a blessing and directed his followers to do the same.

When I realized how often the Bible refers to this concept and when I saw and heard about the phenomenal changes in peoples' lives as a result of receiving a blessing, I began to see what a tremendous concept it is. I began to realize that what I had stumbled onto had the potential of becoming a great and wonderful tool for helping others.

Van Savell, a pastor in Blythe, California, who worked with me on this book, likened this realization to discovering a gold mine. "When you visited me three years ago (in Seattle), you camped in my lounge chair every morning, writing little two-page devotionals for a series you were working on. Every now and then you would stop, pick up your cell phone, and call someone back in Florida, Texas, Georgia, or some other place in the country. You were quick. Few words were spoken, but I picked up immediately that your words were filled with power. I figured out what you were up to, and I liked it. That very week I began the same process. It was liberating to me and life-giving to everyone I called. Just by your example, I had discovered and embraced the process of eulogizing *now*."

Blessing or eulogizing others has proved to be a powerful ministry truth to me and to others with whom I have shared it.

Let's look at some of the Bible passages. Every time the words *bless*, *blessing*, or *praise* appear, they are a translation of the Greek word *eulogy* in one of its forms.

In the New Testament

Early in the New Testament, Simeon gives a blessing to Mary and Joseph concerning Jesus. "Then Simeon blessed them, and said to Mary, his mother: 'This child is destined to cause the falling and rising of many in Israel, and to be a sign that will be spoken against'" (Luke 2:34).

Some other passages in the New Testament that speak of blessing are:

Praise [*eulogy*] be to the God and Father of our Lord Jesus Christ, who has blessed [*eulogized*] us in the heavenly realms with every spiritual blessing [*eulogy*] in Christ.

Ephesians 1:3

The tongue is a little member and boasts great things. . . . With it we bless [*eulogize*] our God and Father, and with it we curse men, who have been made in the similitude of God. Out of the same mouth proceed blessing [*eulogies*] and cursing. My brethren, these things ought not to be so.

James 3:5, 9–10 NKJV

You have heard that it was said, "You shall love your neighbor and hate your enemy." But I say to you, love your enemies, bless [*eulogize*] those who curse you, do good to those who hate you, and pray for those who spitefully use you and persecute you.

Jesus in Matthew 5:43–44 NKJV

Bless [*eulogize*] those who persecute you; bless [*eulogize*], and do not curse.

Romans 12:14

When we are cursed, we bless [*eulogize*]; when we are persecuted, we endure it.

1 Corinthians 4:12

By faith Isaac blessed [*eulogized*] Jacob and Esau in regard to their future. By faith Jacob, when he was dying, blessed [*eulogized*] each of Joseph's sons, and worshiped as he leaned on the top of his staff.

Hebrews 11:20–21

Finally, all of you, live in harmony with one another; be sympathetic, love as brothers, be compassionate and humble. Do not repay evil with evil or insult with insult, but with blessings [*eulogies*], because to this you were called so that you may inherit a blessing [*eulogy*].

1 Peter 3:8–9

In the Old Testament

As you might expect, the Old Testament is full of passages describing the practice of blessing others. Perhaps the main Old Testament truth about this is contained in Numbers 6:22–27:

The LORD said to Moses, "Tell Aaron and his sons, 'This is how you are to bless the Israelites. Say to them:

"'"The LORD bless [*eulogize*] you and keep you;
the LORD make his face shine upon you and be gracious to you;
the LORD turn his face toward you and give you peace."'

"So they will put my name on the Israelites, and I will bless [*eulogize*] them."

Notice the promise of the last line. "They will put my name on the Israelites, and I will bless them." As Aaron and his sons bless the Israelites, they are putting God's name on them as well as God's blessing. Our blessing releases God's intended blessings on others as well as on ourselves.

Here is how the Living Bible puts it:

Now the Lord said to Moses, "Tell Aaron and his sons that they are to give this special blessing to the people of Israel: 'May the Lord bless and protect you; may the Lord's face radiate with joy because of you; may he be gracious to you, show you his favor, and give you his peace.' This is how Aaron and his sons shall call down my blessings upon the people of Israel; and I myself will personally bless them."

In Genesis 49 Jacob summons his sons so he can bless them. He then individually blesses them by name and with specific blessings. Here is the blessing given to Asher: "Asher's food will be rich; he will provide delicacies fit for a king" (v. 20).

And to another son he says, "Naphtali is a doe let loose, he gives beautiful words" (v. 21 NASB).

The passage then concludes with this, verse 28: "All these are the twelve tribes of Israel, and this is what their father said to them when he blessed them, giving each the blessing appropriate to him."

The Value of Blessing

Blessings, which were highly valued in the economy of the Jews, were considered to be predictive, powerful, and very important. Perhaps the most famous story about blessings is the story of Esau and Jacob in Genesis 27.

Isaac was old, and his eyes were dim, the Bible says. He didn't know how much longer he would live, so he called his two sons to receive his blessings. First, he called his eldest son, Esau. Before giving his blessing, Isaac made an unusual request: "Get your weapons—your quiver and bow—and go out to the open country to hunt some wild game for me. Prepare me the kind of tasty food I like and bring it to me to eat, so that I may give you my blessing before I die" (vv. 3–4).

Isaac's wife, Rebekah, overheard her husband's words to Esau. Since she favored her younger son, Jacob, she devised a plan to get Jacob the blessing. Rebekah dressed Jacob in Esau's clothes and "covered his hands and the smooth part of his neck with the goatskins" (v. 16). Rebekah then gave Jacob some tasty food and bread to bring to the elderly Isaac.

In the disguise, Jacob approached his father. Isaac was not sure whether it was Esau or not and said, "The voice is the voice of Jacob, but the hands are the hands of Esau" (v. 22). Jacob came closer and kissed his father. Isaac "caught the smell of his clothes" and blessed him (v. 27).

Isaac began his blessing with these words: "Ah, the smell of my son is like the smell of a field that the LORD has blessed. May God give you of heaven's dew and of earth's richness—an abundance of grain and new wine." Then the blessing continued: "May nations serve you and peoples bow down to you. Be lord over your brothers, and may the sons of your mother bow down to you. May those who curse you be cursed and those who bless you be blessed" (vv. 27–29).

Imagine Esau's anger when he came home and found that the blessing had been given to, or rather stolen by, his brother. "When Esau heard his father's words, he burst out with a loud and bitter cry and said to his father, 'Bless me—me too, my father!'" (v. 34).

Isaac may have been elderly but he wasn't stupid. He knew immediately what had happened. He said, "Your brother came deceitfully and took your blessing." Then Esau asked, "Haven't you reserved any blessing for me?" (vv. 35–36). He was hoping Isaac could come up with a second blessing that would undo the first.

"Isaac answered Esau, 'I have made him lord over you and have made all his relatives his servants, and I have sustained him with grain and new wine. So what can I possibly do for you, my son?'" But Esau wasn't ready to give up. He asked, "'Do you have only one blessing, my father? Bless me too, my father!' Then Esau wept aloud" (vv. 37–38).

Isaac gave Esau what blessing he could: "Your dwelling will be away from the earth's richness, away from the dew of heaven above. You will live by the sword and you will serve your brother. But when you grow restless, you will throw his yoke from off your neck" (vv. 39–40).

As you feel the agony of Esau and hear the mixed blessing his father gave him, you begin to understand how important a blessing was in Old Testament times. It is my understanding that blessings like this are a form of prophecy. The prophecy is not a guarantee but an opportunity that God has given through a Spirit-anointed blessing.

Blessings are also important today. The cry of mankind's heart is still, "Bless me, my father. Speak well of me." We are all looking for that word, that gesture, the magic formula that will make us feel acceptable. We want to know we are a person of worth.

Just before Jesus ascended to heaven, he spoke a prophetic blessing on his disciples, expressing to them the value he saw in them: "But you will receive power when the Holy Spirit comes on you; and you will be my witnesses in Jerusalem, and in all Judea and Samaria, and to the ends of the earth" (Acts 1:8).

Earlier Jesus had told his disciples "Truly, truly, I say to you, he who believes in Me, the works that I do, he will do also; and greater works than these he will do; because I go to the Father" (John 14:12 NASB). This was a promise not only to the disciples but to all believers for all time.

When Jesus committed the future of his church into the hands of his disciples, he was giving to them a monumental blessing and a statement of his confidence in them. Not only was the Great Commission an awesome responsibility, it was a magnificent and precious promise of potential. It was their blessing—and ours!

A BLESSING EXERCISE

What one Scripture in this chapter has special meaning to you?

Francis Frangipane defines a gap as "the space that exists between what is and what ought to be."

There are gaps everywhere and we are very proficient at seeing them and calling attention to them in others while ignoring them in ourselves.

Blessers will get beyond the gaps in others.

SEVEN

WHAT YOU SHOULD KNOW ABOUT BLESSINGS

There are two kinds of blessings: blessings for the present and blessings for the future. Present blessings or eulogies express what is actually visible and true about an individual. They are acknowledgments of what a person is now.

Eulogies for the future express what the person can become because the potential is there. In a real sense they are prophetic and predictive.

Present Blessings

We bless or eulogize people for who they are or for the good we see them doing. We call attention to what is noteworthy in them. Every person has much good about him or her—right now. Of course, we all have bad in us too, but watch out that you do not let the wrong and deficient in others keep you from seeing and praising the good and right in them.

Here are some examples of present-day blessings you can give:

To a child: "John, you are a very kind and unselfish person."

To the lady in the convenience store: "You are always pleasant, and it is a joy to do business with you."

To an employee: "You are a very diligent and faithful person. I appreciate you very much. You are a real asset to the business."

To an employer: "I enjoy working for you and appreciate the consideration and thoughtfulness you give to us as your employees."

To your wife: "Honey, you are very faithful and efficient."

When we focus on the good in others, we will always find qualities and actions that we can praise or eulogize.

Most people are like stray dogs. If you are nice to a stray dog that comes around to your back door, you soon find that he loves you and your house; in fact you can't run the dog off. He is at your back door every day. Although I hate to compare people to stray dogs, you will find that if you make others feel good about themselves, they react in much the same way. They become your friends.

Future—Prophetic—Blessings

There can and should be a prophetic element in eulogies. Hebrews 11:20 says, "By faith Isaac blessed [*eulogized*] Jacob and Esau in regard to their future."

We can give prophetic blessings when, under the leadership of the Holy Spirit, we see the potential in others and tell them about that potential. This can be general (such as saying, "May peace and love be with you always," or "I am confident that God is going to finish in you and bring to completion what he has started"). It can also be specific (such as, "I believe you will be a wonderful wife for some man, and together you will do great and good things in this world for God and others," or "With your sharp mind you will be a first-class engineer"). Such prophetic statements need to be said by faith, and by faith I mean that we declare what we believe God has said to us for another. So we don't speak prophetic blessings without having spent time in prayer and sensing the leading of the Holy Spirit.

God backs the blessings he initiates. God has promised that if we invoke his name, he will bless. Do not forget what the apostle Peter wrote regarding the reward we receive when we bless others: "Finally, all of you, live in harmony with one another; be sympathetic, love as brothers, be compassionate and humble. Do not repay evil with evil or insult with insult, but with blessing, because to this you were called so that you may inherit a blessing" (1 Peter 3:8–9). By blessing others, we inherit blessings for ourselves.

Here are some examples of prophetic blessings, or blessings concerning things to come. Count on the Holy Spirit to guide you in this matter. He will delight to do so.

> To a child: "You are a very thoughtful person, and one day you are going to grow up to be a great mother and wife."
> To a college man: "Son, I have the gift of seeing a winner and you are one." (This is what Professor Tommy in the introduction said to the student, changing the direction of his life.)

To a college woman: "Young lady, you have great potential and are going to be a great artist."

To a creative young person: "John, you are going to become a person who creates many things that will be a benefit to humanity."

Here is a beautiful prophetic blessing that Mary Swope suggests can be given to children:

> In the name of Jesus Christ: Within you dwells the spirit of creativity, for you are made in the image of the great Creator, the Maker of heaven and earth. He is the one who gives you ideas to design, build and perform. Let Him fill your imagination with creative thoughts that, when brought to reality, will bring glory to Him and blessing to others. May the beauty of the Lord our God be upon you to establish the work of your hands.[1]

As you look at people and pray for them, the Holy Spirit will give you things to say prophetically. This is one of the great values in prayer. When Jesus looked at people, he saw things that others could not see. Others would never have given some of these people a chance of becoming the kind of people that Jesus envisioned.

Remember the many prophetic words of Jesus to a bunch of raw recruits—his disciples. He said, "You are the salt of the earth" and "you are the light of the world" (Matt. 5:13–14). It must have seemed like a joke. No one else would have said anything like that; no one else saw anything at all in them. But Jesus did, and these men indeed became "salt" and "light" in this world.

In his first words after the love chapter in 1 Corinthians, Paul expresses the value of future-tense blessings: "Let love be your highest goal, but also desire the special abilities the Spirit gives, especially the gift of prophecy. . . . One who prophesies is help-ing others grow in the Lord, encouraging and comforting them" (1 Cor. 14:1, 3 NLT).

A BLESSING EXERCISE

Look around you. Do you see someone with special potential? Tell the person what you see.

On Christmas Eve, 1769, young Johann Dannecker, while playing in a street in Stuttgart, Germany, knocked to the ground an
elderly gentleman. Rather than reacting negatively to the acci-
dent, the man questioned the boy about who he was and what
he wanted to be when he grew up, and then blessed him with
this challenging and prophetic statement: "Make up your mind
that, whatever you become, you will do something before you
die for which the world will always bless you."

Johann never forgot those words. They were planted in his heart
as a seed. In the course of time he became a famous sculptor,
and his works were found in the capitals of Europe, but he was
never satisfied that any of them met the challenge. Then, on
reading a Scripture portion from the New Testament about Jesus,
he received inspiration and did a sculpture of the Christ.

This fulfilled in his heart the challenge given so long ago. Later
he refused Napoleon's offer to do a statue of Venus for the Louvre,
because, as he said, "Sire, the man who, receiving a divine vision,
makes it the theme of his loftiest achievement would commit an
unspeakable sacrilege if he were to devote his powers to carving
a pagan goddess. My art has consecrated my work."

EIGHT

TWO LEVELS OF POWER IN BLESSINGS

Even when there is (no) special spiritual dimension to it, there is power in praising and blessing others. Praise and blessing give nourishment to our souls. We need this kind of food for the soul just as much as we need physical food for the body. So when people are blessed, the results are good. Just as food meets a physical need, good words meet the soul's need for a full life. While there is tremendous power in blessings on a natural level, there is even more power on the spiritual level.

■ The Soul Level

In his book *The Latent Power of the Soul*, Watchman Nee cautions that there is much we can do without God. Using the right methods, we can have great power with people. Many books have

71

been published showing how salesmen and business executives can accomplish their goals by using the right techniques. *The Right Words at the Right Time* by Marlo Thomas and friends tells stories of many lives that were dramatically changed when the right words were spoken at an appropriate time. The testimonies of famous people like President Jimmy Carter, former first lady Barbara Bush, baseball star Sammy Sosa, and others in the political, entertainment, and business worlds reveal how a few choice words redirected their lives. Each of these people remembered an incident when someone said the right thing at the right time that profoundly affected them.

Corn will grow for an atheist if he does the right things, and it will not grow for a spirit-filled Christian if he does not follow the natural laws of corn growing. This is all right and good, but there is another dimension for the Christian, an extremely powerful dimension. When God becomes involved in our good words, because he initiates them in us, the results are amazing.

■ The Spiritual Level

Jesus said, "Man does not live on bread alone, but on every word that comes from the mouth of God" (Matt. 4:4). What comes out of the mouth of God? When God speaks, you get truth and reality. He sees even before the need is recognized and he sends the provision on its way. Often we are just the timely delivery person speaking on his behalf.

When blessings originate with God and are given under the inspiration and instruction of the Holy Spirit, the divine power of God is exercised. Remember the promise, "If you put my name upon the people . . . I will bless them" (Num. 6:27, author's translation).

Watchman Nee said, "God will back and bless whatever He initiates."[1] This does not in any way negate the natural level; in fact they work together as a double whammy, so to speak.

Remember the stories in the introduction? What did the people in those stories say that made such a profound impact on the hearers?

Debbie's Christmas card simply called attention to a virtue of each person on her team. The words were powerful enough to convince one discouraged man not to quit his job.

Gary's counselor bragged about the good qualities she had noticed in him. Long after he had graduated and become a pastor, Gary decided to honor his former counselor before his congregation and show what this kind of eulogy could do. Her two daughters flew in for the occasion. They told the pastor that no one had ever honored their mother before.

Remember the worker at the private school who called the home of the boy with bad behavior problems? What did she tell the father? She just told him all the good things she had seen in the young man. At the end of the conversation, the father said, "Now, tell me why you have called." She took a long time convincing him that she had called just to tell him good things about his son. There was no other reason at all. I saw her recently and she told me how well this young man is doing.

The manager of the airline office chose not to complain about his worker's bad work ethic. Instead, he complimented him on all the good things he had seen in him. His work ethic changed in three days.

These are just a few examples of how God can use us to speak words of blessing to others. When we are living and walking in and by the Spirit, God will generate in us ideas and words of blessing, even though we may not be conscious that he is using us. Just recently I received a card from a young man who had done some very bad things during a nervous breakdown. He

73

told me how much a phone call I had made to him had meant. He was emotionally down at the time, but I was unaware of it. In fact I did not realize that I was doing anything at all spiritual, although it certainly turned out that way. God used my call to bless him.

If you love the Lord Jesus and are living for him, he will bless even the things you do in your own strength and wisdom, and he will use them in the lives of others. This is true because often he has originated what we do naturally. The difference between a spiritual and natural eulogy is not worth worrying about since it is very hard to make a mistake eulogizing anyone.

When I feel I should bless or eulogize a person who does not like me (or of whom I am not particularly fond), I can be nearly 100 percent confident that the motivation comes from God, for in myself I would have no desire to bless the person. God commands us in his Word: "Bless those who persecute you; bless and do not curse" (Rom. 12:14).

A BLESSING EXERCISE

Ask God for the name of one person you can bless today. Then be sure to bless that person.

PART TWO

HOW CAN I
BLESS OTHERS?

We are blessed and very much so.
We are blessed and then some.
In fact we are too blessed to be depressed.

Quotes collected from various sources

R. C. Chapman, a devout Christian, was asked how he was feeling. "I'm burdened this morning!" was his reply. But his happy countenance contradicted his words.

So the questioner exclaimed in surprise, "Are you really burdened, Mr. Chapman?"

"Yes, but it's a wonderful burden. It's an overabundance of blessings for which I cannot find enough time or words to express my gratitude!"

Seeing the puzzled look on the face of his friend, Chapman added with a smile, "I am referring to Psalm 68:19, which fully describes my condition. In that verse the Father in heaven reminds us that he 'daily loads us with benefits.'"

NINE

DEVELOPING THE ABILITY TO BLESS

Understanding the technicalities of the scriptural teachings on blessings is not as important as putting blessings into practice in our lives. Very few of us understand the inner workings of internal combustion or of television, but that does not keep us from driving a car or watching TV. Scripture warns us of "ever learning, and never able to come to the knowledge of the truth" (2 Tim. 3:7 KJV). Knowledge of the truth is simply learning from the experiences we have through life.

We are able to develop the ability to eulogize when we learn a few laws and follow them. Laws are principles written into the fabric of life that yield rewards for those who obey them and consequences for those who do not obey them.

We live in a world of cause and effect. If you want a certain effect (something good to happen), then find and carry out the cause or causes that will bring about the effect.

To be changed internally, so we can act externally and bless others with ease and joy, there are five laws we need to follow:

The law of the heart
The law of developed sensitivity
The law of deliberate repetition and regularity
The law of the Spirit of life in Christ Jesus
The law of understanding who we are

The Law of the Heart

F. W. Boreham of Australia referred to our heart as the Home of the Echo. What he meant was that what we send out comes back to us. So much of what we see in others is due to what is already in us. The condition of our own heart determines to a large degree what we see in others. Counselors call this projection. If our heart is programmed in the negative, then we will see the negative in others; and if our heart is full of the good and positive, that is what we will see most easily in others.

Ronald Rolheiser tells this story in his book *The Holy Longing*:

> One day a Buddha, badly overweight, was sitting under a tree. A young soldier, trim and handsome, came along, looked at the Buddha, and said, "You look like a pig."
>
> The Buddha replied, "You look like God."
>
> "Why would you say that?" asked the rather surprised and young soldier.
>
> "Well," replied the Buddha, "we see what is inside of us. I think about God all day and when I look out that is what I see. You, obviously, must think about other things."[1]

If we are seeing the wrong and negative in others rather than the good and positive, the condition of our heart needs to be changed. Without this change, we will never be able to see the good in others consistently and naturally and spontaneously call attention to it. It is no wonder that when the old veteran Paul wrote to the young rookie Timothy, he said, "The goal of our instruction is love from a pure heart" (1 Tim. 1:5 NASB).

While we cannot change our hearts ourselves, we can be changed. God is ready to do this, so we can cooperate with him as he works in us. God delights in transforming hearts and renewing minds. Paul said we are transformed (*metamorphis* in the Greek) by the renewing of our minds (see Rom. 12:2). The renewing of our minds is nothing more than reprogramming them with the purity of truth.

Jesus could look at a group of uneducated and rough fishermen and see in them what they could become. This enabled him to call them "the salt of the earth" and the "light of the world." For us to be light and salt requires cleansing—the cleansing promised if we walk in the light (do as we are instructed) as Christ is in the light. We need our hearts reprogrammed—garbage out, truth in. Only Christ can do this through his cleansing blood.

This is the *first law* that helps us give a blessing: *When we concentrate on getting and keeping a renewed heart, our heart becomes pure.*

The Law of Developed Sensitivity

Built into each one of us is a natural law that allows us to develop a sensitivity or insensitivity to anything or anyone. Because of this ability, people who live around airports do not hear the planes, those who live next to railroad tracks never hear or feel trains as they pass, and an orchestra conductor can tell which instrument is out of tune when the whole orchestra is playing. Heightened sensitivity is the reason the University of Florida gave a Ph.D. to an entomology student who could distinguish 225 different kinds of crickets by their sounds and the reason the college professor of one of my grandsons could identify 200 different species of birds by their song.

Seattle is famous for its many views of Mount Rainier. In that city you often hear, "the mountain is out" or "the mountain's not out," referring to the mountain's visibility on a particular day. Only those who notice daily if the weather allows a view of Mount Rainier ever comment on it. Others never notice. This illustrates the law of developed sensitivity.

Another example is coon hunters who can tell their dog by its bark a mile away, and they also know what their dog is chasing at that moment, even if their dog is running with many other barking dogs.

Think of it like this. A young couple wakes up one morning and the husband says, "Wasn't it wonderful? The baby slept all night." The wife says, "You didn't hear anything? Good for you. I got up three times to take care of the baby." Now if you can grasp why the husband heard nothing while his wife could hear a whimper in the next room even though she was sleeping soundly, you can understand why we are sensitive to some things and insensitive or unconscious to others. The mother's heart is tied into the child, and the father's heart knew if he heard something he would have to get up. She had been responding in love to the baby for a long time and had developed this sensitivity. He had confidence that his wife would meet their baby's needs, so he could sleep through the crying.

Here is the law: If we become aware of something, and if we give expression to that awareness in some positive way, then we will become increasingly aware and conscious of that thing in the future. If we continually ignore something when we become aware of it, or if we do not give some outward expression to it, we will soon not be able to notice it at all. In fact, eventually, we will be able to look at it and not see it, or we will hear it and not really be aware of its presence. This law enables us to become very conscious or completely unconscious of almost anything or anybody.

When the man who could hear the crickets was at my house, he pointed out to me a bush that had eighteen different kinds of crickets in it. Though I had passed that bush every day for years on the way in and out of my house, I had never heard a single cricket, or at least I had not consciously heard any. He never listened to a cricket without giving some kind of response to it. I, on the other hand, do not care about crickets. If I think of them at all, I think of them as a nuisance. So I ignore them.

Probably now you see how this applies to our subject. For a long time we have noticed the negative in other people, and often we comment on it. What I am saying is that we can now develop the opposite outlook. We can learn to look for the positive in others. At first, trying to develop this ability will be very hard, but like all habits it comes with practice. Soon it will be a part of our basic outlook. When we remind ourselves to look for the good in another and then comment on what we see, it will become natural and normal for us to do this often. But, remember, habits have to be developed. We must consciously practice looking for positive qualities in others.

When you are getting started, you have to deliberately choose to look for the good in someone else and then comment on what you see. After a while, when it becomes a habit, you will do it spontaneously and naturally.

This is the *second law* that helps us give a blessing: _As we train ourselves to notice the positive things in others and comment on them, we become increasingly conscious of these qualities._

◼ The Law of Deliberate Repetition and Regularity

Regularity is a law of life. What we use, we keep and develop; what we do not use, we lose. If we are living a healthy lifestyle, we will eat and sleep with regularity. Also we will often express to our loved ones that we love them and why we love them. When things are repeated regularly, they empower both the one repeating them and the one who hears them.

This is very true in regard to giving blessings. To the person giving the blessing, it becomes a good habit. Eventually it becomes natural and spontaneous to see and call attention to the good in another.

For the person receiving words of commendation and blessing, it is a reminder of his or her positive qualities, which become a building force in the person's life. Consistent positive reinforcement will convince people of their value and worth in this world.

In Jamaica, where I grew up, many women used to make a living breaking up big rocks into small stones to be used on the roads. They tapped on the big rocks with a very small hammer over and over again until the rock split in two. Then they went to work on the halves and then on the quarters until the rocks were reduced to a usable size. Even as repetitive hammer blows eventually changed the rocks, so consistent eulogizing will eventually transform a person.

A Testimony of a Repeated Eulogy

Penny Riley testifies to the importance of a eulogy: I was alone working in the church kitchen when our pastor came in. He stood in front of me and said, "I thank God for you every time I think of you."

84

I was surprised but very pleased. I responded, "Thank you. How nice!"

He turned and left, but about five or ten minutes later he returned and repeated the same words. I was a little startled because this was the second time he said the same thing, but again I thanked him. He left, and I wondered why he had repeated the words. I knew he was not getting senile. Surely he remembered he had just said the same thing to me.

After another five minutes, he came a third time and repeated the same words: "I thank God for you every time I think of you." This time I did not say thank you. Something welled up inside of me from deep down and I started to cry. My pastor didn't say another word; he just turned and left. At that point I think he knew I had finally received what he had said to me.

That day a change took place in me, a healing deep within. I felt loved and accepted. This has become a permanent part of me now. My heart is warmed and I become emotional each time I think about that day or when I tell about what happened.

I am so glad that my pastor kept coming back. I needed to be loved that day and every day. God knew it and used my pastor to express it.

Processes and Events — Daily Routines

Life is made up of processes and events. Processes are those things we do on a regular basis, and events are those things that happen once in a while. While it is true that events can be exciting and stimulating, it is equally true that we cannot build a life on events. They do add color to life, however. Think of a marriage. Events would be the celebration of birthdays and anniversaries, while the processes would be the routine of each day. In the long haul the process is more important than the special events.

Sometimes, because of past experiences, a person will surround himself or herself with a bad self-image, like an impregnable wall. At first, when positive words are said to such a person, the wall keeps them from penetrating, but if those words are repeated often and sincerely, they will eventually get through and the walls of a bad self-image will slowly but surely be broken down.

Repetition does not mean the words need to be exactly the same. In fact saying the same words over and over would become very mechanical. When positive words vary, they have more of an impact.

If a blessing or praise is given on a regular basis, it will have a powerful effect, because repetition results in reinforcement. It's how things become a part of us. Actions repeated become habits, whether they are good or bad. Ideas become reinforced by repetition and then dominate our lives, whether they are right or wrong. Repeated eulogies will build the positive self-image of an individual.

This is the *third law* that helps us give a blessing: *The reinforcement of actions or words through repetition and regularity develops a habit.*

■ The Law of the Spirit of Life in Christ Jesus

Another law is that of the Spirit-filled, Spirit-guided life. As we live under the control of the Holy Spirit, we will increasingly see things and people as God does, thereby becoming aware of his nudging about blessing or eulogizing others. In addition, he will give us prophetic vision of what is to come and how best to communicate this to others. Jesus always seemed to see the potential of people, like Peter and John, and he called it out of them. Following his example, we can communicate blessing through the leading of the Holy Spirit.

86

God's Spirit will always be building up or edifying rather than tearing down. If we allow our thinking to be renewed by the Spirit of God, then what we say will naturally be a blessing.

The Spirit has come to counsel us, to convict us, to change us, and to teach us, so we can become increasingly Christ-like. Becoming like Jesus internally will cause us to act like he did externally. To be God-centered is to be aware of others in a new way. Then we will act toward them in love.

This is the *fourth law* that helps us give a blessing: *Spirit-filled living causes us to see and love others as Jesus did.*

■ The Law of Understanding Who We Are

The main reason we do not naturally and spontaneously bless other people is that we do not realize how blessed we are as children of God. We are separated from God and this separation has caused us to become dysfunctional. We have developed a basically negative attitude, causing us to focus on the faults of others and of ourselves rather than on virtues and goodness.

In *Life of the Beloved*, Henri Nouwen says, "The blessed cannot help but bless others."[2] We are blessed and then some, but we need to really know this, not only in our heads but in our hearts, before it will cause us to bless others.

The Bible is filled with verses that tell us how special we are in God's eyes, and we need to read and believe what God says. Many of us are quite familiar with Paul's word to Timothy that all Scripture is inspired by God (2 Tim. 3:16 NASB). We may quote it frequently. But are we as familiar with the second half of the verse that says God's Word "is profitable for teaching, for reproof, for correction, and for training in righteousness"? And are we aware that the purpose of God's Word is to make us "adequate, equipped for every good work" (v. 17)?

87

God's Word has a purpose. We are to receive it and experience it, which means that we must read it and believe it if it is ever to perform its work in us. The writer of Hebrews says the word that was heard did not profit "because it was not united by faith in those who heard" (4:2 NASB).

So we must receive what God says about us, which means incorporating the information with faith, if we are ever going to be equipped to bless people. The next two chapters will help us grow in our understanding of our blessedness in Christ.

This is the *fifth law* that helps us give a blessing: *When we know how blessed we are now in Jesus, in spite of our past, we are able to see the good in others and call attention to it.*

A BLESSING EXERCISE

Meditate on each of the five laws, one per day, until your new understanding of your internal condition allows you to give external blessings.

Come, you who are blessed of My Father, inherit the kingdom prepared for you.

Matthew 25:34 NASB

Two days ago I was kneeling in prayer in the front room of our
house at 6:30 in the morning. I'd just confessed sins and was asking God for a blessing that day, needing to feel loved by him.

Our little boy, Timothy, who is twenty-two months old, had
just gotten up, and I noticed out of the corner of my eye that he
had sneaked quietly into the front room. He's always quiet in
the morning when I'm praying because his mom tells him to
be, but this time he ambled straight over to me, put a hand on
my clasped hands, and said, "Hi, special one. Hi, special one.
Hi, special one."

Never once has he called me that before. Six times he called me
"special one." He said it enough for me actually to get it—that
God was speaking to me and giving me a blessing.

Bill White, outreach and college pastor, Emmanuel Church,
Paramount, California

TEN

ACCEPTING OUR BLESSINGS FROM GOD

God has commanded us to love him with all our being. He also commanded us to love our neighbors. Jesus gave a new commandment to believers. He told us to love one another. The New Testament is filled with different approaches to working out this love. The key, however, is not that we love others just because he told us to do so, but because God—who is love—first loved us. Only as we receive his love and exercise faith in his love, will we be able to love as he has and as he commands. When we do this, we will be able to give others the gift of our eulogy.

■ God Has Blessed Us!

"Blessed be the God and Father of our Lord Jesus Christ, who has blessed us with every spiritual blessing in the heavenly places in Christ" (Eph. 1:3 NASB). God has blessed or eulogized us with every spiritual blessing. What does this mean? It means that God has spoken (past tense) over us every spiritual good word that we need. We are blessed fully, right now.

In Matthew's recording of Jesus' comments about the judgment, this issue of God's blessing is enlarged: "Then the King will say to those on His right, 'Come, you who are blessed [eulogized] of My Father, inherit the kingdom prepared for you from the foundation of the world'" (Matt. 25:34 NASB).

Receiving the Blessing

The act of receiving is as definite an act as that of giving. If someone gives a blessing, it must be received before it does any good. It must be taken as the truth, believed, and acted on.

Whether or not a person receives the eulogies given him or her determines their value. If we have a poor self-image (which most of us do), it is very easy to rule out, take lightly, or deny what God is saying to us. But the truth is, when God speaks, that is it—it is a done thing. Making this "done thing" a part of our lives must be our focus.

Remember, God has given us the right to choose whether or not we will receive what he offers us. If we believe what it says in the book of Genesis, we understand that God creates by his word. When we accept what God has said and act on it in faith, that thing is as good as accomplished, because God speaks and it is done.

A BLESSING EXERCISE

Make a list of the blessings you have received from God.

There is nothing I can do to make God the Father love me any more.

There is nothing I can do to make God the Father love me any less.

His love for me is not based on my performance.

This is what grace is.

I have the choice as to whether or not I will receive his love in the ways he chooses to give it.

It is remarkable how easy it is to bless others when you are in touch with your own blessedness.

Henri Nouwen

ELEVEN

ENJOYING OUR RELATIONSHIP WITH GOD

Relational blessings are those blessings that God has spoken over us indicating who we are to him, by him, and for him, and who he is to us. God calls us by many names, all representing the relationships he has with us and those we have with him. These names represent the relationship, position of trust, and responsibility he has bestowed on us. Some of these names are figurative and others actual, but all are very definite and descriptive of what he has made us, how he trusts us, how he values us, and how he feels about us.

▉ Who I Am in Christ (Right Now)

Read aloud the following Scriptures about who we are in Jesus. Then, based on these verses, make the appropriate confessions that follow. (Remember, a confession is simply agreeing with God about what he has said.) I suggest you do one a day, meditating extensively on the blessing. The repetition and the reading aloud will begin to internalize the blessing for you.

A Child of God

Scripture: "How great is the love the Father has lavished on us, that we should be called children of God! And that is what we are!" (1 John 3:1).

Confession: Right now, I am a child of God. He is my Abba Father in heaven. He has given me his life; I am born from above with his quality of life. I was spiritually dead and unable to relate to him. Now, I am spiritually alive and able to communicate, commune, and have fellowship with him as a loved child with a great and good Father.

Beloved (Esteemed, Dear, Favorite, Worthy of Love)

Scripture: "To all who are in Rome, beloved of God, called to be saints: Grace to you and peace from God our Father and the Lord Jesus Christ" (Rom. 1:7 NKJV).

Confession: I am very special to God. I am beloved, esteemed, dear, favorite, and worthy of love. He loves me in such a way that nothing will ever keep him from loving me and giving me his best. Nothing in this world will separate me from his love, in which I am totally and absolutely secure. I am very special to God right now.

Overcomer

Scripture: "Those who receive abundance of grace and of the gift of righteousness will reign in life through the One, Jesus Christ" (Rom. 5:17 NKJV).

Confession: I am an overcomer (a winner in life). By the grace of God I have in me all that is needed to make me a winner in the real sense of the word. I will reign in life and will not be overcome by evil. I am more than a conqueror through Jesus Christ.

Friend

Scripture: "Greater love has no one than this, that one lay down his life for his friends. You are My friends if you do what I command you. No longer do I call you slaves, for the slave does not know what his master is doing; but I have called you friends, for all things that I have heard from My Father I have made known to you" (John 15:13–15 NASB).

Confession: I am a friend of God; he calls me that, and that I am. This means there is a new intimacy with him as he opens his heart to me and asks me to open my heart to him. Proverbs 18:24 says that there is a friend who sticks closer than a brother. Such a friend is Jesus now to me.

Son (a Mature Child)

Scripture: "For all who are being led by the Spirit of God, these are sons of God" (Rom. 8:14 NASB).

". . . that He might redeem those who were under the Law, that we might receive the adoption as sons. Because you are sons, God has sent forth the Spirit of His Son into our hearts, crying, 'Abba! Father!' Therefore you are no longer a slave, but a son; and if a son, then an heir through God" (Gal. 4:5–7 NASB).

Confession: I am a son (a mature child) of God and joint heir with Christ. I have a great future ahead of me. The Spirit of God leads me through life into all truth and reality, so I can choose to live like his mature child. Because I am his son or daughter,

97

God imparts to me responsibilities and privileges. I shall accept all of the responsibilities and avail myself of all the privileges.

Saint

Scripture: "Paul, an apostle of Jesus Christ by the will of God, to the saints who are at Ephesus and who are faithful in Christ Jesus" (Eph. 1:1 NASB).

Confession: I am now a saint (a holy one) by the amazing grace of God. In and by Christ Jesus he has made me holy and given me the Holy Spirit to dwell in me and lead me into all truth.

Heir

Scripture: "And if children, then heirs—heirs of God and joint heirs with Christ, if indeed we suffer with Him, that we may also be glorified together. For I consider that the sufferings of this present time are not worthy to be compared with the glory which shall be revealed in us" (Rom. 8:17–18 NKJV).

Confession: Because I am a child of God now, he is fathering me and giving me all I need in this life, while preparing me for the life to come when I will receive all that will be mine as an heir. Truly the best is yet to come. We cannot even comprehend all the good things that God has prepared for us because we are his children and joint heirs with Christ.

Ambassador

Scripture: "God was in Christ reconciling the world to Himself . . . and He has committed to us the word of reconciliation. Therefore, we are ambassadors for Christ" (2 Cor. 5:19–20 NASB).

Confession: Not only am I a child and son of God, but I have been appointed by him to be his representative in this world, to let others know about him, his ways, his will, and his love. By his grace I will be a good representative in this world on his behalf.

Holy Priest

Scripture: "You also, as living stones, are being built up a spiritual house, a holy priesthood, to offer up spiritual sacrifices acceptable to God through Jesus Christ. . . . But you are a chosen generation, a royal priesthood, a holy nation, His own special people, that you may proclaim the praises of Him who called you out of darkness into His marvelous light" (1 Peter 2: 5, 9 NKJV).

Confession: I am a holy and royal priest with the right and privilege to stand before God and offer up spiritual sacrifices for others and for myself. I will take this wonderful appointment and intercede on behalf of others and myself.

Figurative Names

These are names that the New Testament gives to Christians to indicate how God views us and how he will treat us.

Temple of God

Scripture: "Do you not know that your body is a temple of the Holy Spirit who is in you, whom you have from God, and that you are not your own? For you have been bought with a price: therefore glorify God in your body" (1 Cor. 6:19–20 NASB).

Confession: I am a temple of God. He has chosen to live in me and love me. Christ in me is my hope and guarantee of glory.

Citizen of Heaven

Scripture: "But our citizenship is in heaven. And we eagerly await a Savior from there, the Lord Jesus Christ, who, by the power that enables him to bring everything under his control, will transform our lowly bodies so that they will be like his glorious body" (Phil. 3:20–21).

Confession: I am a citizen of the kingdom of God and heaven; all the privileges of this kingdom are mine here and now. As a citizen I will partake of all the benefits offered to me and accept all the responsibilities.

Body of Christ

Scripture: "Now you are the body of Christ, and members individually" (1 Cor. 12:27 NKJV).

"And he gave some, apostles; and some, prophets; and some, evangelists; and some, pastors and teachers; for the perfecting of the saints, for the work of the ministry, for the edifying of the body of Christ" (Eph. 4:11–12 KJV).

Confession: I am a believer in Jesus and I have become with others the body of Jesus in this world. Together we will manifest what Christ is like so that others can learn to trust him. I am an important part of his body here and now.

A BLESSING EXERCISE

Meditate on these relational blessings, one each day, until you have spent time with them all.

If God had a refrigerator, your picture would be on it.

If he had a wallet, your picture would be in it.

If he had a will, and he does, your name would be in it as a beneficiary.

He could choose to live anywhere in the universe, and he chose to live in your heart.

TWELVE

RECEIVING OUR INHERITANCE FROM GOD

While some of God's blessings are relational, others are experiential. God says it and it is so. In Christ Jesus we have "obtained" an inheritance. Peter described this inheritance as imperishable, undefiled, one that would not fade away, "reserved in heaven" (1 Peter 1:4 NASB).

What has happened to us because God says so? All of the following verses describe blessings that God has spoken about you and me. They are true now and we can appropriate them now. Meditate on one each day as you build up your reservoir of accepted blessings.

memory Verse

Forgiven

Scripture: "If we confess our sins, He is faithful and righteous to forgive us our sins and to cleanse us from all unrighteousness" (1 John 1:9 NASB).

Confession: I am in Christ; in him I am forgiven for my sins, totally, completely, forever forgiven, and they will be remembered against me no more. I am free from all condemnation and free to be all that he made me to be and that he saved me to be.

Justified

Scripture: "But now a righteousness from God, apart from the law, has been made known. . . . This righteousness from God comes through faith in Jesus Christ to all who believe. . . . and are justified freely by his grace through the redemption that came by Christ Jesus" (Rom. 3:21–24).

Confession: By the grace of God I am justified—made right with God and completely acceptable to him right now. By reason of the new birth, I have been made God's child. Jesus became sin for me that I might become the righteousness of God in him (see 2 Cor. 5:21).

Reconciled

Scripture: "Therefore, if anyone is in Christ, he is a new creation; old things have passed away; behold, all things have become new. Now all things are of God, who has reconciled us to Himself through Jesus Christ" (2 Cor. 5:17–18 NKJV).

Confession: By His grace I am totally and completely reconciled to God now and forever. That means that any differences between us, because of my sin, have been settled. If God is for me, who can be against me? He did this for me when I did not care or want him, so what will he do for me now that I am his beloved, chosen child?

Sealed

Scripture: "For no matter how many promises God has made, they are 'Yes' in Christ. And so through him the 'Amen' is spoken by us to the glory of God. Now it is God who makes both us and you stand firm in Christ. He anointed us, set his seal of ownership on us, and put his Spirit in our hearts as a deposit, guaranteeing what is to come" (2 Cor. 1:20–22).

Confession: I belong to God my heavenly Father. He has redeemed me, reconciled me to himself, and set his seal on me so that all may know I belong to him. He has marked me as his own and given me the Holy Spirit as a guarantee of the fact that I am his.

Adopted

Scripture: "Just as He chose us in Him before the foundation of the world, that we should be holy and blameless before Him. In love He predestined us to adoption as sons through Jesus Christ to Himself, according to the kind intention of His will" (Eph. 1:4–5 NASB).

Confession: I am a child of God now. He chose me and adopted me so he could love me. Nothing can keep him from loving me and nothing in this world can separate me from his love and care.

This chapter and the last one do not provide an all-inclusive list of the relational and experiential blessings that God has given to us but will give you some indication of the largeness of his mercy and grace. In all of this he is seeking to let us know who we are in Christ Jesus.

What more could we want or ask for in our relationship with him?

A Blessing Exercise

Meditate on these experiential blessings, one each day, until you have spent time with them all.

The voice that calls us the beloved will give us words to bless others, and reveal to them that they too are no less blessed.

Henri Nouwen

His divine power has granted to us everything pertaining to life and godliness.

2 Peter 1:3 NASB

THIRTEEN

LIVING IN GOD'S PROVISION

God's blessings are provisional. While God has spoken and will fulfill all he has said, it is our responsibility to receive the blessings and act on them. As my children grew up, I blessed them with the promise of a college education. But, although I could help them financially, one thing I could not do was go to college for them. To fully appropriate the blessing, they had to go to college themselves. One of them chose not to do so; as a result that child is without a college education. This is what I mean by a provisional blessing. The blessing is provided to you, but you must receive it before it will have an effect on your life.

God's Provisional Blessings

The following are some provisional blessings or promises that God has spoken over us to meet all the needs we have in this life. Through these we can live successfully, victoriously, securely, joyfully, and triumphantly, thereby bringing glory to him.

He promises to supply all our needs, to hear and answer our prayers, to provide us with wisdom and strength every day, and to give all grace, mercy, and truth for our lives. God has not left anything out. Absolutely nothing is missing.

Look at the following promises. Read and confess them out loud, one each day. There is power when we speak these words to ourselves as well as to others.

Wisdom

Scripture: "If any of you lacks wisdom, let him ask of God, who gives to all generously and without reproach, and it will be given to him" (James 1:5 NASB).

Confession: There is available for the asking all the wisdom I need to make good and right decisions in life. When I need wisdom, I will come to God and ask with the assurance that I will receive. It is my choice to act on the wisdom I receive from God, and by his grace I intend to do so.

All Needs Supplied

Scripture: "And my God will supply all of your needs according to his riches in glory in Christ Jesus" (Phil. 4:19 NASB).

Confession: The Lord is my shepherd; I shall not want. For all of life and for all its situations, God will supply all my needs.

I am content with what he gives, for it is from the heart of a loving, caring Father who always gives me the best.

Strength

Scripture: "I can do all things through Him who strengthens me" (Phil. 4:13 NASB).

Confession: I am continually facing situations in life I do not have the strength to handle appropriately, but, because I have Jesus living in me, his strength is mine and I am able to do all he asks me to do and I am able to do it well.

Victory

Scripture: "But thanks be to God, who always leads us in triumph in Christ, and manifests through us the sweet aroma of the knowledge of Him in every place" (2 Cor. 2:14 NASB).

Confession: Life is full of battles and struggles, difficult situations that are more than I can handle. In and by Christ and his wisdom and strength I will win. I will overcome. I know that victory is not victory *from* battle but victory *in* battle. I am a victor and a winner.

The Privilege of Prayer

Scripture: "Ask, and it will be given to you; seek, and you will find; knock, and it will be opened to you. For everyone who asks receives, and he who seeks finds, and to him who knocks it will be opened. Or what man is there among you who, if his son asks for bread, will give him a stone? Or if he asks for a fish, will he give him a serpent? If you then, being evil, know how to give good gifts to your children, how much more will your Father who is in heaven give good things to those who ask Him!" (Matt. 7:7–11 NKJV).

Confession: My Father in heaven and Lord Jesus Christ have promised to hear and answer me when I call on them in prayer. It is my privilege as God's child to come boldly before him, certain that he will always hear me and show me mercy.

Promise of Answered Prayer

Scripture: "This is the confidence which we have before Him, that, if we ask anything according to His will, He hears us. And if we know that He hears us in whatever we ask, we know that we have the requests which we have asked from Him" (1 John 5:14–15 NASB).

Confession: My Father in heaven will answer all my prayers. While his answer may not be what I wanted to hear, I know it will be the best for me, for he loves me too much not to say "no" or "wait," when that answer is best.

Guidance

Scripture: "But when He, the Spirit of truth, comes, He will guide you into all the truth" (John 16:13 NASB).

Confession: In my life I am faced with many difficult decisions. By the grace of God he will guide me to know the truth of what is best. I choose to listen to the Holy Spirit and follow his guidance.

Deliverance in Times of Temptation

Scripture: "No temptation has overtaken you but such as is common to man; and God is faithful, who will not allow you to be tempted beyond what you are able, but with the temptation will provide the way of escape also, so that you will be able to endure it" (1 Cor. 10:13 NASB).

Confession: Life is full of trials and temptations; it was never promised otherwise. But God's promise to me is that he will always aid me when I am tempted, guiding me in what to do and how not to yield to the temptation or wrongly react to the trials of my life. He will lead me in the paths of righteousness for his name's sake.

Never Forsaken

Scripture: "Let your conduct be without covetousness, and be content with such things as you have. For He Himself has said, 'I will never leave you, nor forsake you.' So we may boldly say: The LORD is my helper; I will not fear. What can man do to me?" (Heb. 13:5–6 NKJV).

Confession: Though I live in a world where broken contracts and betrayals are common, I do not ever have to worry or fear what Jesus will do in his relationship to me. He has promised never to leave or forsake me but to always be there with me and for me. I choose to live in faith, trusting his promise and therefore having no reason to fear.

Peace

Scripture: "Be anxious for nothing, but in everything by prayer and supplication with thanksgiving let your requests be made known to God. And the peace of God, which surpasses all comprehension, will guard your hearts and your minds in Christ Jesus" (Phil. 4:6–7 NASB).

Confession: There are many things around me that could cause me to worry and be fearful, but I will not give in to them. I will take all of my concerns to Jesus, and, as I turn them over to him, he will give me inner, real, and lasting peace in the middle of all storms or other situations of life.

Grace

Scripture: "And God is able to make all grace abound to you, so that always having all sufficiency in everything, you may have an abundance for every good deed" (2 Cor. 9:8 NASB).

Confession: At all times and in every situation, God has promised me the grace that allows me to be and do all I should be and do and the ability to live a life that is pleasing to him. His all-sufficient grace is mine, and I choose to receive it and use it daily.

The Effectual Blessing

Have you received what God has done for you, what he has given you, what he continues to do in you? We must receive God's gift or blessing before it can do us any good. We must take it as truth, believe it, and act on it if we are to realize the blessing's value for us.

This same principle applies when we bless or eulogize others. Whether or not people receive our eulogies is not our responsibility. Even if they do not seem to receive them and in reality do not, we are still accountable for giving blessings and it is to our advantage to do so. However, the person we are blessing will not benefit until he or she receives it.

The gift of prophecy, as defined by Paul, is one way of giving eulogies. He says, "Everyone who prophesies speaks to men for their strengthening, encouragement, and comfort" (1 Cor. 14:3). When writing to the church in Thessalonica, Paul told them, "Do not despise prophetic utterances" (1 Thess. 5:20 NASB). Most preaching on this Scripture has been to warn against refusing the use of prophecy in church services, but the verse applies directly to the issue of eulogies or blessings, spoken by anyone at any time. It means we should not take lightly a good word that is given to us.

A BLESSING EXERCISE

Prioritize these eleven blessings from God with the blessing you're most thankful for at the top of your list. There is no right or wrong order. Use the list to think about all that God has done for you.

PART THREE

WHERE DO I START?

Do not merely listen to the word, and so deceive yourselves. Do what it says. Anyone who listens to the word but does not do what it says is like a man who looks at his face in a mirror and, after looking at himself, goes away and immediately forgets what he looks like. But the man who looks intently into the perfect law that gives freedom, and continues to do this, not forgetting what he has heard, but doing it—he will be blessed in what he does.

James 1:22–25

Dear Pastor,

I have not taken the time to tell you how much I love you and your wife and to say how much you mean to me and the tremendous impact you have had on my life. I have the utmost respect and admiration for you and consider you my spiritual grandparents.

Your Timothy and son,
David Cox

FOURTEEN

SIMPLE WAYS TO GIVE BLESSINGS

M y whole life and ministry were changed one day when I, as a young minister, went fishing with an older man. He said to me, "Today, let me do the preaching." I gladly agreed for he was an excellent Christian and a very wise, practical person. During the afternoon he said to me, "You preachers always tell us what to do but never tell us how to do it."

These words sank into my heart, and their truth began to affect all I did. Through the years I have come to see that my spiritual gifting has been to make the application of truth very simple so anyone can put it into practice. His statement aided me in recognizing that spiritual gift and spurred me to develop it.

As a result, I increasingly find myself asking questions about all truth. How does this truth work out best in life here and now? So here comes the practical end of giving eulogies and blessing others.

Four Things to Remember

First, eulogizing is really very simple. Remember Scripture says that we are to beware lest anyone corrupt us from the simplicity there is in Jesus (see 2 Cor. 11:3). We tend to complicate things. Churches often make the Christian life more difficult than it really is. God has made things simple enough for anyone to do, regardless of education or natural ability. Everyone can learn to speak a few words of praise.

The second thing to remember is that *simple* does not necessarily mean easy. When you first begin, you may in fact find it very difficult to give blessings. This is true of any new endeavor. When you start something new, it is hard to make the adjustment because you are stepping out of your comfort zone into a new area that you have not yet mastered. You are not comfortable doing it, so you can expect to feel somewhat awkward as you start.

Do you remember how uptight you were when you began to drive a car? You had to think about every little thing you did. Now, turning on the directional signals or the windshield wipers comes automatically. You do those things instinctively. Blessing others will come naturally too after a while, but it will take some time.

Third, it is almost impossible to hurt people or make a bad mistake when you are complimenting them. All normal people love to be praised. There is really no danger in doing this, and it is a good way to release the goodness and love of God in this world.

Fourth, when you hear a truth and want to make it part of your lifestyle, it is wise to put it into practice at the earliest opportunity and as often as possible. The Bible speaks of those who are "always learning but never able to acknowledge the truth" (2 Tim. 3:7). Don't just learn about blessings; make an effort to practice the truths in this book. It is important for you not only to agree with what has been written here but also to put it into practice.

The journey of a thousand miles starts with the first step. So let's go.

■ Three Basic Ways to Give a Blessing or Eulogy

For blessings and eulogies to be meaningful, they have to be communicated, not just thought or felt. Praise is ineffective if you just think it; you have to express it. Therefore, words, articulated in one way or another, are the means by which blessings are given. Here are three basic ways to communicate blessings.

Face-to-Face

The first way to communicate blessings is face-to-face—looking a person in the eye and speaking with all sincerity. If it is appropriate, place your hand on the person when talking to him or her. Touch seems to be very important in such communication. It is generally accepted that love is communicated in five ways—through quality time, words spoken, gifts given, touch, and service. When we touch a person as we speak a blessing to him or her, we are communicating love in two important ways.

Sometimes a blessing may come spontaneously; other times you will have thought through what you want to say ahead of time. The more you bless others, the more spontaneous it will become. Increasingly you will see the truth about another person and will be able to tell him or her about it.

Remember, while you may feel uncomfortable speaking a blessing, the person you're speaking to may also feel uncomfortable. People often have a hard time accepting a compliment. There are reasons for this. Since they have not had much opportunity to practice receiving praise, they may not know how to respond to it. In addition, they may have a poor self-image, making it hard to believe what you say. So, often, they will respond in a negative way. Even so, most of the time, they will not forget what you said in complimenting them, and your blessing will do good. If you sense their discomfort, make your blessing short and to the point. Don't wait for a response from them. Smile, so they know you are sincere, and move on. It is our job to love and eulogize whether or not the praise is accepted.

Sending a Blessing

As beginners, many of us have a hard time looking people in the eye and telling them how much we appreciate them. If you find this difficult to do, you may want to begin by sending a blessing in a card, letter, or e-mail. Sometimes this is the best way, because cards, letters, and e-mails can be read over and over. Instant replay, if you please. My wife and I have letters we call keepers. They are so good and uplifting we read them whenever we need some extra encouragement. A written blessing communicates the thought and effort that went into it.

Without a doubt the nicest blessing I have ever received from someone outside of the family is this one from army chaplain Major Ken Revell. He began his letter to me in this way:

To a man who has moved me towards God,

To a man who has inspired me to love Jesus,

To a man who has challenged me to live a pure life,

To a man who helped me to understand grace,

To a man who helped me see Jesus in a clearer way,

To a man I hope to be like some day, at least in Spirit.

Cards and notes happen to be my favorite way to give a blessing. I have actually designed four cards that have a short printed message on the front and have space inside to write the blessing to the particular recipient. See the illustrations of these cards on pages 126–129. Copy and use them yourself, or design your own and keep a supply handy. You can also purchase appropriate cards in card shops and Christian bookstores.

The first three cards are the ones I send to most people, but of course it depends on the circumstances and their spiritual needs. We must be sensitive to what will be meaningful to each person. Some people would not respond positively to the last one.

By Phone

The third way to give a blessing is over the phone. Again, this may be easier than having to look a person in the eye. By phone we can contact people at a distance, with little effort and time required.

Because of my travel schedule, I frequently find it convenient to bless people over the phone. The cell phone has enhanced our ability to reach out and touch people at a moment's notice. This makes it imperative that we be tuned to the prodding of the Holy Spirit about the needs of others. When he brings people to mind, we can immediately phone them and give them a blessing.

125

I

was thinking of

You

and giving thanks.

JUST
WANTED
YOU
TO KNOW...

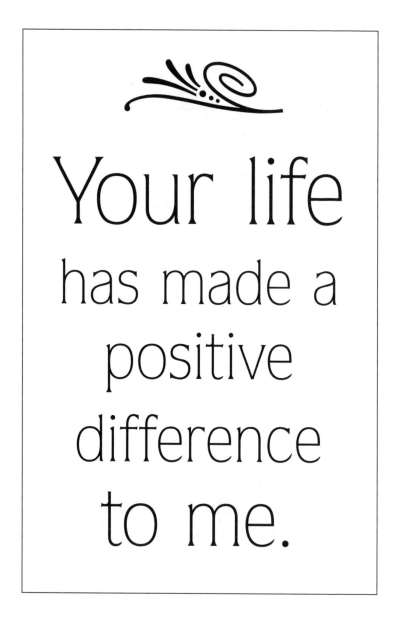

Your life

has made a

positive

difference

to me.

I bless you for...

I bless you with...

The Lord bless you and keep you:
the Lord make his face shine
upon you and be gracious to you:
the Lord turn his face toward you
and give you peace.

Numbers 6:24–26

INSIDE

In the
name of
Christ
Jesus
I bless
you.

FRONT

I received this letter from a young man who had recently graduated from college and was depressed about the way his life was going:

> I do not know if you remember calling me around November of 2000, but I was really depressed because things had not gone too well, and I thought for sure I would never have a real job again. In short, I felt abandoned by God. Well, one morning you called me and blessed me and told me that I was going to be fine. I look back at that three-minute phone call as a turning point, because from that time onward things got significantly better. Thank you. In short, thank you for treating me like a human being when society wanted to throw me away.
>
> *Micah*

Remember the verse: "Let no unwholesome word proceed from your mouth, but only such a word as is good for edification according to the need of the moment, so that it will give grace to those who hear" (Eph. 4:29 NASB). I suggest you memorize and meditate on this verse. It will prompt you to become a blessing machine.

A Blessing Exercise

If you have taken the time to do the chapter exercises and meditated on the Scriptures and confessions, then you probably find yourself already developing a habit of blessing. Thank God for what he has done.

Do not wait for extraordinary circumstance to do good; try to use the ordinary situations of life.

Jean Paul Richter

We practice daily what we believe; all the rest is just religious talk.

FIFTEEN

HOW TO BEGIN AND
WHAT TO SAY

Begin your blessing endeavors with your family. The cobbler's kids may be without shoes, but why should your family members be without your blessing? Jesus commanded us to love our neighbors, and the word *neighbor* in the Scriptures means near ones. Who is nearer to us than the people who make up family—parents, partner, children, and grandchildren?

Many of us are guilty of ignoring the positive qualities of those closest to us while doing and saying good things to complete strangers. Think of how kind you are to the stranger who knocks at your door for one reason or another. Sometimes we fail to show the same kindness to members of our own family.

Why not start with a simple thank-you? One woman testified how her home was changed when her husband began to say a simple thank-you for the small things he had taken for granted for years. One thing he told her was, "You know, honey, I have a magic drawer. Every time I open it, I find clean underwear and socks."

Small children are especially vulnerable to negative input, since they have tender hearts. Like little seeds, words fall into those hearts, and you may not know what the harvest is for years. To small children, parents are the most significant people in their lives; they need praise from their mother and father. This can be done in many ways: eulogies done on the spur of the moment; blessings that are appropriate on special occasions, like birthdays, anniversaries, graduations, or special accomplishments; a blessing party. Regular praise is very important to reinforce truth in children, and parents appreciate the blessings of their children also.

Older members of the family need to be blessed, for they often feel that they have wasted their lives and no one really cares about them anymore. I tell young people that if once a day they will eulogize their parents for one thing, they will find that during the first week, their parents may think the children are on drugs, but after that the parents will want to give the children anything they want. To be honest, I don't remember ever blessing or eulogizing my father.

After learning to praise your own family members, learn to bless the people you see on a regular basis—the people you work with and those who serve you, such as waitresses and cashiers at stores. Some people who have very menial jobs are very receptive to compliments and blessings. When was the last time you praised your trash man or mailman? Don't forget to praise people at church, particularly those who do work that is often overlooked. Remember to thank ushers and nursery attendants for the faithful and good service they perform. In many ways they are as essential to a worship service as the person singing the solo or giving the message.

134

As you wait to check out in the grocery line, start thinking of what you can say to the cashier or bagger. When you go to work, think of how you can bless the janitor. While I was in the process of writing this chapter, I went to the grocery store. The cashier had one of the most elaborate hairdos I ever remember seeing. I made a positive compliment about it and asked how long it took to have it done. She replied, "Four hours." The following day when I went to the store again, she said to me, "You made my day yesterday." What an easy way to make someone's day!

It is good to bless or praise even a person whom you may see only once in a lifetime. Such words from a complete stranger lift morale.

Knowing What to Say

Some blessings come naturally. When you love a person, you find that desires rise up in your heart for them, and you wish for them to have the best of everything. True love always has insights into the other person and their potential. Say what you feel. It doesn't have to be elaborate—just a few words, expressing what you desire for your loved one, are sufficient.

You can also find something to say from your personal observations of the person and your insights into his or her character. The more contact you have with others, the more you will observe things about them that you can bless. As you see all the good things they are and do, you will have ideas of what to say.

Generally you will call attention to acts of service, express gratitude, and remark on quality traits that you have seen. Behind every action there is a character trait. One of my daughters-in-law always cleans up after meals with us. The action is noteworthy, but the quality of character that causes the action is really more important. So, in addition to thanking her for helping with the dishes, I often say, "You are a very thoughtful person."

One way to eulogize others is to repeat to them a promise or promises of God. All the promises of God are his desires for his children, so we can bless people with a particular promise that will be fulfilled in their life and experience. An example of this would be: "I bless you with the ability to see the power of God in you in all situations of life, and the ability to release that power for his glory and the blessing of other people."

You may have heard good things from others about a person in your life. When we love someone, we will be very alert to all the things others say about him or her. In blessing another, you can praise these traits, abilities, or potential, perhaps making the individual more aware of them. An example of this would be, "John, everybody who speaks of you talks of your gentleness and kindness." We are all blessed when we know that others are thinking well of us and talking about it.

You can bless someone by speaking about the desire of his or her heart. As we are around others, we can detect the good desires of their heart and ask God to bless them with the fulfillment of their desire. For instance, it is perfectly normal for a person to want to get married and have a family. On hearing this desire expressed, we can then bless the person by saying that we believe God will fulfill this heart desire (see Ps. 37:4).

Expect the guidance of the Holy Spirit in your desire to bless others. One of the real values of prayer is in intercession, praying for others. Often in prayer the Holy Spirit will let you see people as God sees them. You can then bless them with this revelation of God for them and their future. Here are some simple examples:

John, in praying for you, I sense from God a great and useful future with many people being blessed through you.

Susan, as I hold you up before our Lord and God, I always get the picture of the great mother you are going to be.

Bill, thanks for sweeping the driveway. You did a great job. God will use your industriousness.

Mary, you have the loveliest smile in the world. Through your friendly disposition, God will be able to bless many people.

Remember, if the positive is not expressed, the negative is easily assumed. Any good or positive blessing lifts up another person.

Giving a Eulogy or Blessing Party

There are special occasions when it would be very good to give a party, eulogizing the honored person. Times like anniversaries, special birthdays, or accomplishments like graduation or retirement are great opportunities for eulogy parties.

Here are some suggestions for making this a very meaningful time. I'll use the occasion of a child turning sixteen.

The people who will participate: Much planning will go into the party but none is more important than the people you ask to participate. This should include those who know the person well and love him or her, such as family, family friends, the honoree's friends, the pastor of the church, and other significant people in the child's life. These people will speak words of blessing at the party.

You will need to explain to them what is going to be done and how it is going to be done. Remember, most people do not understand the idea of blessing or eulogy at all and have never practiced it, so give them some examples. Then ask them to write out what they are going to say, so the person being honored can keep it as a memory of the blessing and the occasion.

Planning the time: Schedule the party far enough ahead so those you invite can place it on their schedule. Set a date, time, and place.

Plan for food: It can be a full meal or just light snacks or dessert, but make it very special.

Arrange the room appropriately: A good way to arrange the room is to put the chairs in a circle with the person being blessed sitting in the middle. Then all can see the honored person and lay hands on him or her if appropriate.

Have a plan: The following is a proposed schedule for the event.

Welcome the guests.

Have the eating time first.

Formally gather the people together.

Remind them of what is going to happen and why.

Read some appropriate Scriptures, such as Numbers 6:24–26.

Pray specifically for the person being honored.

Sit the young person in a chair in the center of the room.

Have each person stand over him or her and pronounce the blessing.

Have them give the honoree the written blessing.

Thank God for his promise to fulfill the blessings and to bless the blessers.

A Blessing Exercise

Bless each of your immediate family members in the next twenty-four hours. Write down what you say. Then repeat the blessing in writing within a week.

138

CONCLUSION

SIMPLE YET POWERFUL WORDS

Andor Foldes was a skilled pianist at sixteen, but he was struggling. One of the great pianists of his day, Emil von Sauer, the last surviving pupil of the great Franz Liszt, came to Budapest. He asked that Foldes play for him. The young pianist obliged with some of the most difficult works of Bach, Beethoven, and Schumann. When he finished, von Sauer kissed him on the forehead. "My son," he said, "when I was your age I became a student of Liszt. He kissed me on the forehead after my first lesson, saying, 'Take good care of this kiss—it comes from Beethoven, who gave it to me after hearing me play.' I have waited for years to pass on this sacred heritage."

The story is told of the woman who asked her husband, "Do you love me?" He responded, "I told you I loved you when I married you. If it ever changes, I'll let you know."

Ouch! That hurts. Like that husband, most of us often fall into the trap of living on the basis of our past actions, instead of making them fresh today.

Our hearts hunger for a fresh blessing—daily. Like God, we want to hear thanksgiving. We want to receive praise. And we need blessing. Every normal person wants to be blessed. I've found that the way to get a blessing is to give a blessing. The law of the harvest comes into play here.

You reap what you sow.

You reap more than you sow.

You reap later than you sow.

That is what this book is all about—awakening us to the necessity of speaking a eulogy to people while they are alive and showing how simple it is to bless people on a daily basis. We bless, knowing that we will also be blessed in return.

Blessings are simple—and powerful. They change lives. So let's make a difference in someone's life today and give a blessing.

Notes

Chapter 1 The Discovery of This Truth

1. Bill Ligon, *Imparting the Blessing to Your Children: What the Jewish Patriarchs Knew* (Brunswick, Ga.: The Father's Blessing).
2. Bill Glass, *Champions*, P.O. Box 761101, Dallas, 75376-1101.
3. Dr. Mary Ruth Swope, *Bless Your Children Every Day* (Swope Enterprises, P.O. Box 1290, Lone Star, Texas 75668, 1-800-447-9772), 14–15.
4. Ronald Rolheiser, *The Holy Longing* (New York: Doubleday, 1999), 132.

Chapter 7 What You Should Know about Blessings

1. Swope, *Bless Your Children*, 45.

Chapter 8 Two Levels of Power in Blessings

1. Watchman Nee, *Release of the Spirit* (Indianapolis: Sure Foundation).

Chapter 9 Developing the Ability to Bless

1. Rolheiser, *Holy Longing*, 239–40.
2. Henri Nouwen, *Life of the Beloved* (New York: Crossroad, 1992).

Peter M. Lord is a nationally known speaker and pastor. Author of several books, he is best recognized for *Hearing God*, which has sold more than 130,000 copies and helped thousands of men and women grow closer to God. He lives in Titusville, Florida.